STANLEY
PORKCHOP

* This is a true story

It is not often that life changes so much in a single day. But for two lonely blind dogs named Stanley and Porkchop, one hot August afternoon became a day when *everything* changed.

On that ordinary Tuesday, after Stanley's typical breakfast, after his usual afternoon romp in the grass and during his routine mid-day nap, the extraordinary happened. Stanley met his best friend, Porkchop.

Stanley was born blind. He was an odd mixture of Australian shepherd and border collie and sported a dark brown saddle of fur across his back, a white stripe running down the middle of his orange face, a furry white chest and a curtain of thick tan hair hanging down from his tail. Stanley was a handsome fellow and, despite being blind, he enjoyed his first months of life rolling around and playing with his mother, brothers and sisters, who were always nearby. The barn where they all lived was cold at night, but they huddled together to keep warm. Stanley was very content.

Many happy weeks rolled by and Stanley grew taller, heavier and stronger. When the time finally arrived for Stanley and his siblings to start lives with new human families, every puppy in the litter was soon adopted, except for Stanley. It seemed that no one wanted to adopt a blind dog. Not long after, to Stanley's dismay, his mother was also taken away from him.

Stanley now found himself alone, sad and confused and he cried, hoping that someone would pay attention to him. Every day, as was his odd habit, Stanley would raise his head upward, his long snout pointed to the sky. He would then walk about cautiously, his nose poised like a submarine periscope, hoping to catch the smell or sound of another dog or person who might want to play with him.

A couple of weeks later, when it became clear that no one would adopt him, Stanley was brought to a local animal shelter. But, as luck would have it, some nice people from a dog rescue group saw Stanley and quickly took him out of the shelter. They brought him to a busy foster home for dogs where he would be safe. Many dogs of all sizes and shapes lived at the foster home and all the dogs at Stanley's new home could see except him. Even so, Stanley tried to make friends and play whenever the other dogs would let him.

Stanley soon began to notice that most of the dogs arriving at the foster home stayed for only a short time before they were adopted and then gone. Stanley remained because no one wanted a dog who could not see.

The woman who ran Stanley's foster home was very kind to Stanley, but she was also very busy and did not have much time to play with him. Stanley often felt lost, confused and isolated in his dark world.

Then, one morning, the nice woman lifted Stanley onto the front seat of her car, and they embarked on a long journey. Stanley enjoyed the trip, happily riding in the front passenger seat listening to country music on the radio. He was petted frequently, ate tasty snacks and napped with the nice woman close by. Stanley did not yet know that he was traveling to another state to join his new family but it had turned out that someone DID want a blind dog after all!

When he finally arrived at his new home, Stanley met two very nice people and four other canines named Lupe, Alex Marie, Ozzie and Ziggy. The other dogs were older than Stanley and he soon found that they did not want to play with an energetic and roughhousing puppy. Because of his blindness, Stanley often ran headlong into the other dogs and mistakenly stepped on their tails, paws or ears. As a result, the other dogs became a bit wary of Stanley and kept their distance.

Even so, Stanley was happy. He played with his many toys, chewed on bones, sticks and rawhide and ran around the grassy yard in big circles, where there were no obstacles to bump into. He sniffed under the bushes and took long naps in the comfy spot behind the reclining chair. All the dogs in Stanley's pack could wander around a fenced yard whenever they wanted and Stanley quickly learned to use the doggie door to go in and out of the house.

Stanley looked forward to his daily routine. In the morning he ate breakfast and at noon, each dog was given a frozen hotdog or marrow bone to enjoy. There was an evening walk and occasionally a guest with dog treats would liven up the house. Stanley happily joined the pack when they found something to bark at, even though he couldn't see what had caused all the fuss. He loved to drink from the cold water in the fishpond and sniff for crumbs on the patio table. Even so, there were times at home when the dogs just didn't have a lot to do.

During those quiet periods, each of the dogs chose his or her own activity.

Lupe, a large black and white spotted dog who was the pack leader, often chose to enjoy a break from her duties as the boss. She would plant herself in the middle of the lawn and quietly watch the birds, insects, airplanes, leaves, quail and roadrunners. There always seemed to be something that attracted her quiet gaze.

Alex Marie and Ozzie both loved to hunt. The two constantly searched for blue-eared lizards and would team up to guard both sides of a bush or rock, waiting with intense concentration for the creature to emerge. The lizards were far too smart and fast, however, and Alex Marie and Ozzie could never catch one. But they never tired of trying.

Ziggy, meanwhile, enjoyed sitting at the large picture window in the den, on the wide wooden sill, watching the activity on the street and in the driveway. Ziggy watched cars, trucks, people, squirrels, cats and even an occasional hawk that liked to perch in a nearby tree. If anything seemed amiss, Ziggy would sound the alarm, barking a warning to the other dogs. Ziggy was quite proud of his job as the pack's head security guard.

Stanley on the other hand, couldn't do any of these things. He couldn't watch people, animals or cars, he couldn't chase lizards in the yard and sitting at the window was quite pointless since he couldn't see what was outside. So, Stanley often became bored.

As time went on, Stanley spent more and more time during the day sleeping behind the reclining chair, perhaps enjoying dreams of doing what sighted dogs could. Stanley still played with his toys, enjoyed his frozen hotdogs and marrow bones, and loved the attention he received from the humans around him. Yet, something was missing from Stanley's life. He just didn't know what.

Then, on that previously noted hot August day, as Stanley was lazing behind the big chair dreaming, he was surprised by a strange canine nose touching his own. By smell, sound and feel, Stanley could tell this was a very odd-looking creature. The dog had very short and stout legs supported by enormous outward pointing feet. He had a long body that was higher in the rear, an upward curving tail, a rather narrow snout and huge pointed ears. The new dog could walk right under Stanley's belly without touching him! His name was Porkchop. "Where did this little dog come from," Stanley wondered.

Porkchop's upbringing was similar to Stanley's. Porkchop was born blind, in a litter of sighted puppies. He was short and long, and looked like an odd cross between a basset hound, a chihuahua and a bull terrier. Porkchop had short fur and was entirely tan, except for the dark brown tips of his tail and ears. He was full of energy and personality and had a toothy grin, but still no one wanted to adopt him because he was blind. Soon all of his siblings had left for new homes, leaving him all alone.

Porkchop was soon taken to the local animal shelter by his owner because it appeared no one was going to adopt him. However, a kind woman quickly noticed Porkchop and brought him into her home. The woman was very nice to Porkchop, and he loved her, but she operated a rescue for bigger dogs and didn't have much time to spend with him. Because Porkchop was so small and the other dogs so large, and because he was blind and the other dogs sighted, the woman worried about Porkchop's safety around these dogs. Finding himself isolated and alone most of the time, Porkchop became sad and bored, longing for other dogs with whom he could play.

Time went on this way until one day, when he was about two years old, Porkchop was placed in a car by some nice people. Like Stanley had a year before, Porkchop enjoyed a long car ride. He stuck his head out the window to feel the cool breeze, rummaged around the car floor for crumbs and curled up next to one of the warm passengers for a long nap.

When Porkchop finally arrived at his destination, he became very frightened. There were new people and voices, an unfamiliar house and yard, other bigger dogs and lots of barking. But as he cautiously explored his new home, sniffing and listening, Porkchop found that one of the dogs, a quiet gentle one, seemed very interested in meeting him. His name, of course, was Stanley.

In fact, Stanley was immediately drawn to Porkchop. The little dog did not growl or bark at Stanley, but prodded him with his nose, trying to draw Stanley into a game of wrestling. Soon, too excited to wait any longer, Stanley gave in.

Grabbing each other gently with their mouths, rolling around onto their backs and playfully pawing each other, Stanley and Porkchop came to love their new game. Soon, the two wrestled frequently, the matches sometimes lasting an hour or more. After their crazy tussles, which sometimes took them all over the house and yard, Stanley and Porkchop would lie down, panting and exhausted, ready for a nap. Once awake, though, the two would often begin wrestling again.

Stanley and Porkchop made up other games too. They chased each other across the lawn, carefully listening for the other's panting. They dug big holes together in the dirt and sand and played tug-of-war with anything they could find.

As time went on, Stanley and Porkchop came to spend most of their waking hours together. In fact, when Porkchop was beyond Stanley's smell and hearing, Stanley would cry out to the smaller dog. Porkchop would then trot over to good-naturedly nuzzle Stanley. As he stuck his nose in Stanley's ear, Porkchop seemed to whisper to the larger dog, "No worries, friend, I'm here!"

Now, while Ozzie, Lupe, Alex Marie and Ziggy continued to pursue their favorite afternoon pastimes, Stanley and Porkchop had a pastime of their own. It was clear to anyone watching that these two blind dogs were best friends. What they couldn't see, they could feel, hear and smell. They took naps together, explored the yard together, sniffed around the bushes together and were never far apart. While there were many activities they could not enjoy as blind dogs, they made up for it with games of their own invention. And each was comforted knowing his best friend was always nearby.

It is true that neither Porkchop nor Stanley would ever see each other. They would not know each other's fur color or recognize how the other wagged his tail. Yet, none of this mattered to them. Rather, the two once unwanted, unhappy and lonely blind dogs had discovered something much more important..... that true friendship does not require sight, only understanding, acceptance and love.

To this day, Stanley and Porkchop continue to happily wrestle with each other for hours and hours.

*THE END

STANLEY AND PORKCHOP
friends forever

CPSIA information can be obtained
at www.ICGtesting.com
Printed in the USA
FSOW03n0811230616
21900FS

9 780997 029000